IF GOD BE FOR US

PASTORAL REFLECTIONS OF FAITH AND FAMILY CONCERNING THE BLACK CHURCH

BY: DR. M. KEITH MCDA

D1495363

PRESS

If God Be For Us
Pastoral Reflections of Faith and Family Concerning
The Black Church
by Dr. M. Keith McDaniel Sr.

Printed in the United States of America

ISBN 9781628716009

www.xulonpress.com

To Rev Brent
Stay Blessed

For My Family

For The Body of Christ

TABLE OF CONTENTS

~INTRODUCTION~

This written work is rooted in my pastoral reflections of faith and family. In my personal experiences as a Christian and in my professional experiences as a pastor, I have learned a great truth. That truth is this, if God be for us who can be against us? Obviously, this revelation comes from the words of Paul found in the book of Romans (see Romans 8:31). I am convinced that our today is simply a collection of our yesterdays. We are who and what we are today because of the active presence of God in our lives. When God is for you, who can be against you?

What a joy to know that God is for you. Have you ever stopped to consider that God is for you? Have you ever stopped to consider what it means to be favored by God? Isn't there a certain calmness that comes with the knowledge that there exists no power able to withstand the purpose of God? Trying to stop the plan and purpose of God is like trying to hold oil in the palm of your hand. Eventually it will escape your grasp.

This written work is rooted in my belief that God is pro-family. God desires to see families whole and healed. God desires that husbands love their wives and that wives love their husbands. God desires that children honor their parents and that parents teach their children.

This written work is rooted in my belief that the church is God's premier institution of change in the world. Although the church is flawed and imperfect, God still works through the church to change the present age. The church is the body of Christ. Christ is the head of the church. As long as the world turns, the church must see to it that it remains God's agent of change in the world.

This written work is rooted in my belief that both family and faith are constantly attacked by a real enemy. That real enemy is Satan, who does everything he can to destroy our faith and our families. Yet if God be for us, He is more than the world against us.

This written work is rooted in my love and appreciation for the black church and the black family. As I see it, the black church and the black family are the legs upon which all of the black community stands. It is my prayer that as you read this written work you will come to understand the power of reflection and how God's favor is at work in mysterious ways to navigate people of faith in their participation in His plan and purposes.

~CHAPTER ONE~

A DIVINE APPOINTMENT

A life without reflection is one void of understanding. It is God's desire that each human being reflect upon his or her life. It is in the moment of reflection that we are able to examine our stewardship, challenges and accomplishments in an effort to discover where and how God has been active in our lives. After vigilantly reflecting on both my life and my career as a pastor, I have become graciously aware of just how good God has been to me. The presence of God is not always a spiritual mystery. God has demonstrated His presence in my living through the people He has placed in my life, particularly through the pastoral influence of the Black preacher.

I was born in the city of Winston-Salem, the fifth largest city in the state of North Carolina. My mother, a teenager by the name of Branelsia Kay McDaniel was the youngest of four preacher's kids. She gave birth to me on a Sunday morning. To be more specific, I was born at home. On one occasion, I asked my mother who delivered me, and her answer was,

"God." On the morning of my birth, my grandmother, Ivey Nelle McDaniel, took both her daughter and her new grandson to the local hospital. When Dr. A. H. McDaniel, my grandfather, went to church to preach that Sunday morning, he announced that his youngest daughter had just delivered a baby boy and that they were both doing fine. Afterwards he began to preach the gospel of Jesus Christ. My introduction to the world happened in the very moment of preaching. The first person to speak publically for me was my grandfather, my preacher, my pastor, the Rev. A. H. McDaniel. He was instrumental in providing a Christian home that nurtured and protected the gift of God which was buried within my heart.

While instrumental in providing a Christian home, he was also a major religious leader in the community. He understood that evangelism was an essential part of being the church Christ called into being. A. H. McDaniel served as pastor of Union Baptist Church in the city of Winston-Salem, North Carolina, for forty-seven years. From 1933-1980, he preached with passion and ministered to the lost. Hundreds of souls were saved, and over the years Union Baptist became a major component of spiritual and social renewal in the city.

It should be mentioned that when my grandfather became pastor of Union Baptist, the church only had eight members. The story is often told that the first offering collected under his leadership was $1.50. This amount was exactly enough to pay the week's rent. The church experienced significant growth and achievement under his pastorate, including but not limited to purchasing its first property, erecting a new sanctuary, completing an educational wing and a parking lot expansion in 1975 at a cost of $115,000.[1] This was a giant step forward from a $1.50 offering. Like the Apostle Paul, God wrought miracles through the ministry of A. H. McDaniel.

On December 23, 1980, my grandfather passed away from prostate cancer. Despite the fact that A. H. McDaniel passed away over thirty years ago, it amazes me that people can still talk about him for hours at a time, many years after his death. It is without a doubt that his ministry touched their lives. He was a giant in the ministry and impacted lives in a way that I hope to duplicate.

The next pastor to play a significant role in my life was Rev. Dr. B. F. Daniels. In the tenth month of 1981, Union Baptist called Dr. B. F. Daniels as their next pastor. He would pastor Union Baptist for the next sixteen years. It was under his pastorate, at the age of six, that I was baptized into the Christian faith. I gave my life to the Lord after attending a week of Vacation Bible School. One of the deacons extended an invitation to Christian Discipleship on the last night of the week. I heard the voice of the Lord and responded to the invitation by walking to the front of the church. What happened next was amazing. Six or seven other children of the same age came to the front of the church. They, too, desired to know the Lord Jesus Christ.

B. F. Daniels was extremely influential in my life. Daniels would often call on me to read scripture or to say a prayer

---

[1] Union Baptist Church, "Church History," http://unionbaptistwsnc.org (accessed June 5, 2008).

during a worship services while I was very young. My mother would often give me a crash course in pulpit etiquette. She would say things like, "Sit up straight. No talking. No playing. And don't fall asleep." Little did I know that these were the first courses I would take in pastoral ministry.

While Rev. Daniels would create opportunities for me to be a participant in worship, he was also active in areas of my life outside of church. He helped me get my first job. One of Rev. Daniels' favorite restaurants was a local ice cream shop. Dr. Daniels and the manager were good friends. When I was old enough to work, Rev. Daniels gave me the needed recommendation for my first job. Once the manager knew I was a member of Rev. Daniels' congregation, I was hired immediately.

B. F. Daniels understood that the call to pastor individuals includes being concerned about their development outside the walls of the church. God used B. F. Daniels to bring me into the kingdom of God. However, God also used Daniels to bring me into economic and social awareness by aiding me in the area of employment. B. F. Daniels' offering of a recommendation of employment in letter and in person suggested that B. F. Daniel was able to use his influence as a pastor to connect a member of his church to economic resources within the community. B. F. Daniels passed in November 1997. However, his legacy of pastoral influence lives on.

The third pastor to influence me was the Rev. Dr. Sir Walter Mack Jr. In 1999, the Lord blessed Union with its next pastor. Dr. Mack brought a new energy and a new excitement to the congregation. The first conversation I had with Dr. Mack took place in his office. When I came into Dr. Mack's office on a Sunday morning and introduced myself as the assigned worship leader for that morning's worship service, my journey to the pastoral ministry began. When Dr. Mack greeted me, the first question he asked him was, "Are you in the ministry?" My answer was, "No." That was about to change.

Over the course of the next ten months, the Lord took me to higher levels of trusting in His voice. I was being called to the gospel ministry. The Rev. Dr. Sir Walter Mack Jr. was instrumental in helping me discern this call and began to mentor me through my preparation for ministry. As God continued to reveal His will for my life, Dr. Mack encouraged me to enter into a season of prayer and fasting. His influence on my life was such that he helped me discern my call into the preaching ministry and the need to prepare professionally for this calling. Under Dr. Mack's guidance, I preached my first sermon on July 21, 2001, at Union Baptist Church in the city of Winston-Salem. The title of my first sermon was, "An Unchanging God!" Four years later, in 2005, I was called to pastor my first congregation, the Elon First Baptist Church of Elon, North Carolina. Dr. Mack instilled in me the importance of trained clergy. It is because of him that I completed a bachelors, masters and doctorate degrees.

Three pastors, A. H. McDaniel, B. F. Daniels and Sir Walter Mack Jr. all shaped my perspective of pastoral ministry. A. H. McDaniel gave me the spiritual and evangelistic component of pastoring. B. F. Daniels helped me to understand the role of pastor and the importance of helping people live better in community. Sir Walter Mack Jr. helped me transition into ministry through educational preparation. As a result of their influence on my life, I was given a pastoral model that reaches outside of the pulpit ministry.

In the winter of 2009, I was called to pastor the Macedonia Missionary Baptist Church, in Spartanburg, South Carolina, the second church I have served in my pastoral career. It was in the month of December. I was having dinner, eating Japanese food, when I received a call from one of the deacons of the Macedonia church family. His name is Deacon Robert Brewer. He called me and told me that I was the newly elected pastor of this great and historical church. I was tremendously humbled. Despite the fact this was a Baptist church, and that Baptist churches work on a call system, I truly believed it was a divine appointment orchestrated by the hand of God.

I was first introduced to Macedonia four years earlier. I was invited to Macedonia to preach a youth day service. One of the Deacons, Deacon Charles Jeffers, contacted me and inquired if I would be willing to come and share a word from God at a youth program there in Spartanburg. As we talked on the phone, he said that he was given my information from someone else who had heard me preach. He stated that his daughter knew me, even though her name did not sound familiar to me. He went on about me coming to share with Macedonia. I had never heard of him or the church and was confused about how he came to know me. I was shocked to learn that somebody from South Carolina had heard of me, a young preacher from another state.

As the date approached for this preaching assignment, communication stalled between me, Deacon Jeffers and the current pastor of the church. I called several times and no one returned a phone call. I assumed the event had been canceled. It was a Saturday evening about 6pm when my phone rang. It was Deacon Jeffers. He asked if I had made it to Spartanburg yet, and that the church was looking forward to me preaching in the morning. I informed him that I was still in North Carolina and that no one had returned any of my phone calls concerning the details of lodging. Nor had anyone phoned me from the church with further instructions for preaching. He ensured me that everything was a go and that I should get in the car and drive the three hours to Spartanburg. Shortly after hanging up with Deacon Jeffers, the pastor of Macedonia Missionary Baptist Church called me and confirmed. I packed a bag, got in my car and drove three hours to Spartanburg, South Carolina. I arrived approximately at 9pm on a Saturday night. I called the pastor and I called Deacon Jeffers to let them know that I had arrived and was eager to minister in the morning.

That Sunday morning when I got to the church, Deacon Jeffers took one look at me and instantly started to panic. Again, I did not know Deacon Jeffers. He was the one who seemed to know me via our previous phone calls. I later found out that all the while he was calling me and putting the program together, he thought he was talking to somebody else. My shock and confusion over how a church in South Carolina had heard of me was cleared up; they had not heard of me. I was contacted by accident. Nevertheless, I preached that Sunday morning.

What was human error was actually a divine setup. To this day, I remain grateful that Deacon Charles Jeffers forgot a name and contacted the wrong person. This is one case where mistaken identity was a blessing in disguise. Four years later, in 2009, I was called to pastor Macedonia. I accepted the call to the pastorate and delivered my first Sermon on the first Sunday in February 2010.

Macedonia Missionary Baptist Church is an African-American congregation with a rich history. The church was organized in 1894 and received its charter in 1904. Throughout the church's 120-year history, God has richly blessed her. Like most churches, Macedonia has come through many valleys, shed many tears, experienced years that were better than others, but through it all God has kept her. I am currently serving in my fifth year as pastor of this great church, and this written work is a reflection of prophetic ministry and pastoral observations of the church, the community and the country. I am convinced that my calling to this congregation is in fact a divine appointment.

What is a divine appointment? A divine appointment is when God causes a series of events to take place in your life that force you to show up at a particular place, at a particular time, to do a particular work. Everything God does, He does with purpose. Oftentimes when God is orchestrating such an appointment in your life, it is not discernible until the purpose is revealed. When God schedules your divine appointment, you have no choice but to show up on time.

Consider the woman at the well (see John 4). She had a divine appointment. Jesus needed to go through Samaria, not so much for the route but for the appointment. Consider the apostles who were given the command to wait in Jerusalem until they received power (see Acts 1-2). That was a divine appointment. They waited there until the Holy Ghost showed up and endowed them with power. Consider Paul on the road to Damascus (see Acts 9). That was a divine appointment. Jesus showed up in Paul's life that day and completely turned it around. God is always active in our lives, guiding us to see and understand and do His will.

I continue to be convinced that God has a plan for every human life. In His own timing and in His own way, He will make that plan known to those who are willing to walk by faith and not by sight. God does not want to keep His plans hidden from people of faith. He wants us to be aware of His will for our lives. Knowledge of God's will for our lives allows us to live with purpose, with passion and with power.

~CHAPTER TWO~

WHY I LOVE
THE BLACK CHURCH

The Black church grew out of the horror of slavery and the evangelistic efforts of the slave owner and the slave trader. "Black churches were one of the first tools slave masters used to socially engineer Black people."[2] While this is a reality, W. E. B. Du Bois adds to this by stating that the Negro church influenced the Negro's home in America. He outlined this reality in his work *The Souls of Black Folk*. Du Bois saw the religious life of the Negro church as a platform for true articulation of oneself and his/her place in the world. When describing the black church of the early twentieth century, Du Bois stated that, "The Negro church of to-day is the social centre of Negro life in the United States, and the most characteristic expression of African character."[3] Du Bois believed, as do I, that the black church is the recognized midpoint of black

---

[2] Claud Anderson, *PowerNomics, The National Plan to Empower Black America*, (PowerNomics Corporation of America, Inc, 2001), 225

[3] W. E. B Du Bois, *Souls of Black Folk: 100th Anniversary Edition*, (New York, NY: Signet Classics, 1995), 213.

life in America. It is where black people share information, where they fellowship, where they are educated and where they worship.

The Black church is without a doubt the most influential institution that has shaped the progress of Black people to date. Through many dangers, toils and snares, the Black church continues to be the cornerstone of the Black community. In my opinion it is the most important institution of the Black community. In this chapter, I wish to share with you why I love the Black Church.

THE PREACHING

The preaching in most black churches is the climax of the worship experience. The music, the fellowship, the building itself may draw worshipers to the church. However, there is something about the preaching that keeps them coming back. I love the preaching of the black church tradition. "Black preaching uses energy and spirit to take the Word of God and bring it to life in a way that changes lives. It demands that the hearer listen, think, and respond."[4]

The pastor is the person up front during the Sunday morning service. People have come to be inspired and informed. They come to hear a word from the Lord. People don't come to church to talk about their hobbies, their vacations or their social life. They come to church to hear a word.

---

[4] William H. Crouch Jr. and Joel C. Gregory, *What We Love About the Black Church,* (Judson Press, 2010), 3

There is great responsibility given to the preacher to preach the word of God to the people of God.

Preaching is an audacious task. The gospel that is proclaimed by the preacher is also needed for the preacher. Real preaching does not happen without the preacher first preaching the message to himself. Before a preacher stands to declare *thus says the Lord*, the preacher should have wrestled with the text; the text should have ministered to him or her before attempting to minister it to the people of God. Pastors are teachers, and we should be careful and mindful of what we teach our congregations.

Preaching is not a science. It is an art form. It is rooted in personality, theology, experience and context. The art of black preaching is a gift ordained by God. Black preaching at its finest is vivid, dramatic and uninhibited. Black preaching wrestles with the text, argues with the text and then finds celebration in the text. Some preachers are anointed such that as they preach you could close your eyes, and it seems as if you were watching a movie or as if you were really in the text yourself. Some preachers are gifted such to the point that they have us sitting on the edge of our seats.

Black preaching is determined to make every text about Jesus. Whether Old or New Testament, a black preacher is going to talk about Jesus Christ and the crucifixion. It is the narrative, the storytelling, of black preaching that makes Jesus Christ live. Making Jesus live makes the whole Bible come to life. Black preaching has the ability to resurrect an ancient text and make it relevant for a post-modern world. "Christianity begins and ends with the man Jesus—his life, death, and resurrection. He is the revelation, the special disclosure of God to man, revealing who God is and what his purpose for man is. In short, Christ is the essence of Christianity."[5]

As a pastor, I really do believe that every sermon speaks to somebody in a profound way. Every sermon may not produce a shout. It may not produce a dance. It may not produce any outward or visible response from the people. However, I am convinced that every sermon was for somebody. God's word will not return to Him void. It will be deposited in the heart of at least one worshiper, and at least one worshiper will declare it as the word of God for his or her life.

A pastor is more than a maker of sermons. He or she is a counselor and spiritual advisor. Therefore, preaching is a means of pastoral care. It is the truth of God's word, presented to the people of God in the moment of preaching, that liberates the hearer and the doer of God's word. While many within the Black community may not be open to psychotherapy, they will come to church and receive logos-therapy. There are many people who need but will not access professional counseling. However, they will come to church. They will sit in a pew or a choir stand or even a pulpit and receive instruction, counseling, understanding all from the word of God. That is why I love the Black Church.

---

[5] James H. Cone, Black Theology & Black Power, Orbis Books 1997, 34

ITS ROLE IN EDUCATION

From its earliest formation, the black church took a special interest in the education of its congregation and members of its community. Black Christians have always been willing to support education. Whether through local associations, national conventions or personal commitments, black Christians have understood education as a means of liberation in this country. The greatest example of this is the black church's commitment to Historically Black Colleges and Universities (HBCU).

It is important to the note that Historically Black Colleges and Universities throughout the country have strong connections to the black church and the black community. The Baptist Churches in North Carolina organized Shaw University. The AME church founded Wilberforce University in Ohio. The CME church founded Lane College in Tennessee. These institutions were established to ensure that newly freed slaves and their children would have an opportunity to access higher education in this country. Many congregations and associations within the Black Church support local HBCU through rallies or even allotted funds within their budget.

The HBCU helped to meet the need to educate African-Americans in this country. This need was supported by the black church. It was not until the Civil Rights Act of 1964 that blacks were allowed to enter into other institutions of higher education. Prior to this point, Blacks who attended college went to all-black schools. "But when predominately

White schools were forced to open their doors to students of all races, these institutions became interested in the talents of Black athletes and began to recruit Black students."[6] As a consequence, more and more Black students began to attend traditionally white institutions. Nevertheless, the black church is committed to the HBCU. This is why I love the Black Church.

THE CELEBRATION

The worship experience is a significant authority within the African-American community. "The remarkable power of black worship makes possible our discerning a way through life's opportunities and its darkness by faith that always sees a star of hope."[7] The black worship experience is significant because it is an environment where head and heart knowledge of God comes forth. Sermons, songs and prayer are the primary means by which this takes place. The participatory element of black worship is the essential ingredient in creating such an environment. Worshipers are not bystanders, but full participants in everything that happens in worship. "The black worshiping congregation has always been, and continues to be today, a key participatory habitation for Christian nurture that engages us in probing, naming, and

[6] John Corbitt, *Black Churches Reaching College Students*, (West Berlin, NJ: Townsend Press, 1995), 6.

[7] Anne E. Streaty Wimberley, *Nurturing Faith & Hope* (Cleveland, OH: Pilgrim Press, 2004), xiii.

forming images and beliefs of God."[8] It is nurturing because the worshipers are drawn into the narrative in such a way that the biblical story becomes their story.

The Black Church, by and large, believes in giving the Spirit time to do what the Spirit needs to do. Oftentimes you will hear a worship leader pray, "Have your way Holy Spirit" or "We welcome your presence into this place" as a sign to the Lord that the atmosphere is welcoming to the empowering presence of the Lord. In the Black Church there is a celebration of the goodness of God that is like no other! People don't mind giving the God the glory.

The Black Church is a place of empowerment. Empowerment is what Black people strive for, and celebrate when it is achieved. Whether it is empowerment of emotions, finances or relationships, it is often celebrated in the sanctuary of the Black Church. "Freedom in worship and to worship may be one of the hallmarks of the black church experience."[9]

The shout, the dance, the waving of hands, the testifying, the singing, the preaching, the praying are all examples of celebration in the black church. It is not simply emotion void of intellect. It is not simply behavior void of theology. There is a saying often heard in the Black Church: "When I think about Jesus, and all He's done for me, when I think about Jesus and how He set me free, I can dance, dance, dance all night!" The celebration is rooted in knowledge, faith and experience

---

[8] Ibid., 6.

[9] William H. Crouch Jr. and Joel C. Gregory, *What We Love About The Black Church,* (Judson Press, 2010), 43

that all gives way to thanksgiving. So many people have hit some of life's hardest places, yet God has proven Himself to be their redeemer and they don't mind saying so. That's why I love the Black Church.

~CHAPTER THREE~

IS BLACK THEOLOGY RELEVANT FOR THE TWENTY-FIRST CENTURY?

As I see it, The Black Church has always been a moral compass for this country. Issues of civil rights, sexism, racism and cultural identity are so connected to Black folk's interpretation of the gospel of Jesus Christ that these social issues have become theological issues. It is through a personal encounter with Jesus that a person truly comes to understand the work of God and how God desires to be involved in the affairs of human living. The gospel of Christ declares that God is with us, that He is actively working things according to the good and fighting against all forces that seek to make humanity captive (see Romans 8:31).

Black Theology was formulated to strengthen black love and black self-worth. Black bodies were undervalued and systematically taught their souls were depraved from the moment their feet touched American soil. The African slave was not an Englishmen. "Since he was not an Englishmen, his importance and his place in the Englishman's scheme of things was predetermined."[10] This predetermined placement of the black body and the black soul was considered inferior to that of White bodies and the soul of White persons. Black Theology, therefore, served as a call for black love. "Jesus' work is essentially one of liberation. Becoming a slave himself, he opens realities of human existence formerly closed to man."[11] James Cone, the leading voice in Black Theology for the 20th century said, "In Christ, God enters human affairs and then dies with the oppressed. Their suffering becomes his; their despair, divine despair."[12]

For most of the 20th century, the political principles of civil rights and Black power were central to the shaping of Black Theology and the Black Church. The ideals of family, spirituality and social responsibility were core values for those of my parent's generation and even the one before theirs. It seems that my generation, those who came of age in the 1980s and 1990s, have more of a focus on wealth and material consumption than any other generation of those who consider themselves the descendants of American slavery. Hip Hop defines my generation over and above the social issues of yesterday. Hip Hop is such a defining presence in Urban America that

---

[10] C. Eric Lincoln, The Racial Factor in the Shaping of Religion in America, in African American Religious Thought an Anthology edited by Cornel West and Eddie S. Glaude Jr. Westminster John Knox Press 2003, 161
[11] James H. Cone, Black Theology & Black Power, Orbis Books 1997, 35
[12] Ibid, 36

many are beginning to view it as a religion. A few years ago, Jay-Z and Kanye West released a song called No Church In The Wild. The song pushes one to question the relevance of church and theology. This moves me to raise the question, "Is Black Theology relevant for the 21st century church?"

What is Black Theology? The purpose of Black Theology is to analyze the nature of the Christian faith in such a way that black people can feel good about being Black. There are many who no longer feel this is necessary. Black Theology is the study of God's movement, God's concern and God's desires for the oppressed and marginalized within the Black community. It is a theology that does not ignore or disregard the plight of Black people. It is a theology that affirms blackness. While this is so, it is not a theology that is anti-white.

The notion of blackness is not simply a reference to skin color, but a symbol of oppression that can be applied to all persons of color who have a history of oppression or marginalization for any reason. Racism is about the control of wealth, power and resources. However, as Anthony B. Bradley says, "Black liberation theologians seek to apply theology in a manner that affirms the humanity of blacks in ways that they believed were previously denied."[13] It is a theology that begins in oppression, seeks affirmation and has an ultimate goal of liberation.

The Bible and the cultural context have always been the necessary ingredients for forming an effective theology for

---

[13] Anthony B. Bradley, *Liberating Black Theology: The Bible And the Black Experience In America*, Crossway Books 2010, 18

Black folks. Enslaved Africans identified with the biblical story of the Hebrews enslaved by Egypt. Moses represented a liberator of those in bondage, one who was inspired by God to set the people free. The pharaoh for the slave was the slave master. Egypt for the slave was the plantation and the institution of American slavery as a whole. Furthermore, they believed that the God of the Bible was still active in the unfolding story of human history. The biblical story of Jesus also connected with slaves. Slaves noted both the suffering humanity of Jesus, as well as Jesus' ability to set the downtrodden free.

The biblical story must be relevant within the context and culture in which one lives. What are the issues that plague the United States of America today? Immigration, gun control, jobs, housing, health care, same-sex marriage, globalization— these are the issues that seem to drive much of the political agenda and posturing of our current context. What does Jesus say about these issues? How do these issues impact the Black community and the Black Church?

As I read scripture I see that human freedom was and will always be the essence of Jesus' ministry. His ministry was rooted in God's love for the world. John 3:16, one of the first verses of scripture I learned, simply tells us that God loved the world, and because He loved the world God gave the world His son. His son was given as a gift, a gift given for the sole purpose of freedom. James Cone once said that there is no liberation independent of Jesus' past, present and future coming.

No greater man has ever lived in this earth than Jesus Christ. No single life has ever meant has much too so many people that Jesus of Nazareth. Christianity was born in the mind and the heart of Jesus Christ a man born into a minority class of people. He was a teacher, a preacher and a thinker. His people experienced the pain of the dominant culture. "In 63 B.C. Palestine fell into the hands of the Romans. After this date the gruesome details of loss of status were etched, line by line, in the sensitive soul of Israel, dramatized ever by an increasing desecration of the Holy Land."[14] The psychology of Jesus' ministry is such that he taught the people how to survive and thrive in the midst of the harsh realities forced upon them.

Jesus' ministry targeted both the oppressed and the oppressor. Jesus' death and resurrection was the ultimate expression of restoration. The resurrection of Jesus Christ serves notice that injustice and oppression never have the last word. The resurrection of Jesus serves notice that the experiences of life should not have enough authority to destroy the dreams of a human being.

While Jesus is no longer physically on this earth in His person, He is in the Earth through the body known as the Church. Black Theology is still relevant for the 21st Century church. Despite the fact that America has elected and re-elected a Black president, Black Theology is still relevant. Despite the fact that the Southern Baptist Convention has elected it's first Black president, Black Theology is still relevant.

Black Theology is still relevant because the Black Church needs to do a self-test. Black Theology must do the work of

---

[14] Howard Thurman, *Jesus and the Disinherited*, Beacon Press 1976, 18

examining how the Black Church addresses issues of oppression outside the walls of the church but in some cases has failed to address issues of oppression inside the walls of the church. In many ways, the Black Church has used Scripture to oppress members of its own congregation in the same way slave masters used it to oppress Africans in American slavery. Black Theology must do the work of exploring sexism, homophobia, and classism within the Black Church.

Black Theology is still relevant because there is a need for those who live in poverty, those who have limited access to the marketplace of education and healthcare, to have the privilege of accessibility to God. Jesus is the God of the ghetto. That's right. Jesus is the God of the ghetto. What does that mean? It means that Jesus is the God that poor people recognize. It means that Jesus is the champion of the oppressed. It means that Jesus is the one with whom poor people share their frustrations, their joys, their victories and their disappointments. It means that Jesus is concerned for the least of these. It means that Jesus is not anti-success, but He is the voice for those who have no voice.

In the gospel account according to Matthew, Jesus shares an interesting position on salvation and judgment. Matthew 25:31-46, records the words of Jesus as it relates to the care of the poor, the naked and the hungry. In this story some are welcomed into eternal joy. Some are condemned into eternal judgment. Their reward or their punishment is all based upon how to they treated the poor. More specifically, how they treated Jesus. According to Matthew 25:31-46, the presence of Jesus is always with and in the least of these.

Jesus is the God of the ghetto. What does that mean? It means that Jesus is not afraid of crime, disease, suffering, poverty, statistics, stereotypes, racism, sexism or any other *ism*. Jesus came to give humanity life. John 3:16 says, "For God so loved the world that He gave His only Son, so that everyone who believes in him may not perish but may have eternal life." John 10:10 says, "The thief comes only to steal and kill and destroy. I came that they may have life, and have it abundantly."

Jesus is the God of the ghetto. What does that mean? It does not mean that God does not care about the middle class. It does not mean that God does not provide upward mobility and afford opportunity of migration from the inner city. Jesus being the God of the ghetto means that those to whom poverty is a memory should never forget from where God has brought them. It means that because of your journey, when you succeed more, you should enjoy it more.

Black Theology is still relevant because there is still a need to liberate, educate and empower Black minds. We as a people have gained more control, awareness and cultural creation, and we have improved our collective identity. However, more formation is needed. Many issues within the black community still need significant theological inquiry. Issues such as absent fathers, HIV/AIDS, same-sex marriage, teen pregnancy, building healthy blended families and drug addiction are still in need of sufficient theological inquiry and application.

Black Theology is still relevant because the ghetto is still the mission field for the Black Church. While many denominations within the body of Christ are reaching out to Spanish speaking countries, third world and even countries in Africa, there are still far too many within Ghetto America who have yet to learn of the saving power of Christ. There are too many families who are barely surviving, and not enough families who are thriving. When I was growing up, we used to talk about what we wanted to be when we grew up. Now, children are wondering if they will grow up at all.

Black Theology is still relevant because there is still a need to narrate black history. One of the reasons why a call to action is seldom heard in the black community today is because there is a lack of historical knowledge being transferred. "In the church, there are no limitations that can be imposed upon the curriculum by any accreditation agency. There is no need to allocate time for the study of other ethnic groups as an act of political correctness."[15] Black Theology must tell the story of how we made it over.

There is much need to reposition the Black Church as the moral voice, the spiritual headquarters and the collective identity of the Black community. In many of our churches, a demographic is missing. Why are young adults distancing themselves from the Black Church? Why is it that younger Black families are not attending church? Black theology is still relevant because the Black Church needs to reintroduce itself to its own people.

---

[15] Marvin A. McMickle, *Preaching to the Black Middle Class*, Judson Press 2000 , 46

There are millions of Black people throughout this country who have not stepped foot in a Black church outside of a funeral or a wedding. Most pastors preach to the same people every Sunday. We offer Christ to the same families every Sunday. Again, the church needs to reposition itself as the moral voice, the spiritual headquarters and the collective identity of the Black community. This is why Black Theology is relevant.

Black Theology is not separate from Christian Theology. "Black Theology is Christian theology precisely because it has the black predicament as its point of departure. It calls upon black people to affirm God because he has affirmed us."[16] Black theology holds the possibility for a truly religious community to come into existence. It is a theology of resurrection. The resurrection of self-worth and the healing from cultural trauma continues to be the hope of Black Theology. It is the hope of Christian Theology.

---

[16] James H. Cone, *Black Theology & Black Power*, Orbis Books 1997, 118

~CHAPTER FOUR~

THE BLACK CHURCH CONCERNING MARRIAGE, DIVORCE AND REMARRIAGE

There are many institutions within the black community. The Historically Black Colleges and Universities, black owned business, fraternities and sororities, and social clubs are just a few of the institutions that constitute the fabric of the black community. However, my pastoral reflections are centered on two very important institutions within the black community: the Black Church and the black family.

In my opinion, the black church must provide guidance and solutions for the crises of the black family. The black church must do more than shout, dance and have good worship. It must be the premier institution in producing and promoting healthy black families. The stability of the black church is rooted in the stability of the black family. They work hand in hand. Black families have seen improvement in the area of finances and other measurable social successes. However, when it comes to marriage and family, the state of the black community is still struggling. Consider the following statistics:

❖ Nearly half of black Americans have never married, the highest percentage for all racial groups.[17]

❖ Nearly 10 million black families lived in the United States in 2007. Twenty-one percent of these families were married couples with children. This is the lowest of all racial groups. The U.S. average is 32.4 percent.[18]

❖ Although blacks make up only 13.6 percent of the U.S. population, blacks account for 50.3 percent of all diagnosed cases of HIV.[19]

❖ Seventy-two percent of black mothers are unwed.[20]

MARRIAGE

Christian marriages are designed to reveal the presence of God in the family. Have you ever considered that God wants to be a part of your family? Family is important to God. Therefore, family life should be important to us. All families have challenges and issues that threaten to destroy the family's strength and sustainability. However, it is God's desire to

---

[17] Article appeared on http://www.theroot.com/views/poor-state-black-families 3/18/13

[18] Ibid

[19] Article appeared on http://www.blackloveandmarriage.com/2011/02/the-atlanta-post-on-8-important-statistics-black-america-should-pay-attention-to/ 3/18/13

[20] Ibid

see families operating with divine favor and purpose. Family is the first institution ordained by God. Before God created the church, before God gave Moses the law, before God established grace through Jesus Christ, God ordained the family. Family is important to God.

Marriage is an institution ordained by God. God created us as social beings. We were never intended by God to live without the companionship of another person. When couples come to me for premarital counsel, I usually ask them why they want to get married. I always worry when their answer does not have love as its foundation. Obviously, marriage must be more than love. Marriage is about commitment. Some people marry because they have children. Others marry because they see it as the natural progression of being together for a long time. Some marry out of obligation to some moral or ethical rationale. While all of these may be good reasons to marry, if people do not truly love one another and are willing to commit to one another, they may simply end up with a wedding and never a marriage.

A marriage is a covenant relationship between a man and a woman. It is the God-ordained union between husband and wife. This covenant is spiritually binding, as well as legally binding. The word "covenant" is one of biblical significance. When God sought to enter into relationship with His people, He always established a covenant (see Genesis 17:10-11 and Exodus 24:3-8). Covenant relationships are meant to be life-long relationships. That is why in most vows you hear the phrase "til death do us part."

It is important to note that there is a difference between a wedding and a marriage. A wedding is a ceremony. A marriage is a journey. A wedding may consist of a bride, a groom, a preacher, a ring, a dress, a gathered people to witness the exchanging of vows. A marriage is the shared life experience of truly becoming one.

It is possible to have a wedding and never a marriage. A wedding is a matter of finances and planning. In order to have a wedding you must be able to financially facilitate the ceremony. A marriage is a matter of the heart. In order to have a marriage, you must be able to emotionally and spiritually facilitate the journey of becoming one. Unlike the wedding, marriage is not a one day event. It is a journey of leaving and cleaving. It is about leaving one's biological family in order to create one's own family. Marriage is also the constant challenge of leaving one's own self in order to cleave to the one you have married. It is the journey of learning how to forsake others and how to keep yourself for the one with whom you shared vows.

I am of the opinion that before you have a wedding you should already be married. What does that mean? I am simply saying that before you make the investment in a wedding, a one-day event, you should have already made a commitment to the journey of becoming one. Again, marriage is a matter of the heart. A wedding should symbolize to others the commitment already shared between a man and a woman.

God has high standards for marriage. The wedding is the moment in which you make the commitment public. It should not be the moment when you make the commitment itself.

Consider this, we do not baptize persons into the faith then ask them to commit to Christ. Their baptism is the appropriate response to their commitment to Christ. I believe the same should be true with marriage. The wedding should serve as a public confirmation that a commitment to love and cherish one another has already been made. The ceremony should never be more important than the commitment. Marriage is more important than the wedding.

Marriages do not suddenly come into being with a wedding. There was a process that took place before the wedding: Dating, interaction with potential in-laws, evaluation of compatibilities and chemistry. Hopefully, it was also approached with a lot of prayer. Some people fall in love with tremendous intensity. Others seem to ease into the martial relationship bit by bit. Nevertheless, marriages do not come into being out of the blue. Nor are they suddenly perfected because of the wedding. Marriage should be viewed as a lifelong journey.

A Christian marriage requires that you hold two sets of hands. You must hold your spouse's hand. Secondly, you must hold to God's unchanging hand. The Bible says that one person can be overpowered, that two can defend themselves, but a three-strand cord is not easily broken (see Ecclesiastes 4:12). Christian marriages work best when we understand ourselves as yielded vessels through which God can love the other. In other words, it is not really me loving my wife, it is God loving my wife through me. It is not really my wife loving me. Rather, it is God loving me through my wife. Wow! Isn't that radical ?

43

Imagine the grace of God that would be realized if we took this position continually in our marriages?

DIVORCE

Unfortunately, all marriages do not last until death parts the couple. Many marriages are dissolved because of divorce. Everyone does not make a good selection in choosing a life mate. All too often the choice comes down to what a person looks like on the outside as opposed to what he or she looks like on the inside. The true beauty of a wife is not in her hair, her makeup, her shape or her shoes. It is in her heart, her soul and her mind (see 1 Peter 3:3-4). The true strength of a man is not his in muscles or his money, but in his ability to honor his wife and to love his wife without bitterness (see Ephesians 5:25-28 and Colossians 3:19). The Black church needs to help the Black family reinvent what beauty is and where beauty is, so that better decisions are made as they relate to choosing a life mate.

Divorce is painful emotionally, socially and relationally, as well as legally. When going through a divorce, there are many emotions that you have to deal with. You may find yourself struggling with anger, depression, embarrassment and guilt. I can personally testify concerning the pain of divorce. When ten years of marriage ended, I found myself having to deal with the pain of divorce. It was painful to watch people pick sides and it was difficult to listen to people talk about things of which they knew nothing. To say the least, divorcing and pastoring was a whirlwind. Nevertheless, I survived. To God be the glory.

While God views marriage as a covenant agreement, He does allow certain reasons for divorce. Let me be clear: God created marriage. He did not create divorce. Humanity created divorce. The scriptures record an instance where the Pharisees came to Jesus with a question concerning divorce. Is it lawful for a man to put away his wife for any reason? Jesus' response is extremely interesting. He does not immediately deal with divorce. Rather, he begins by explaining marriage. It seems that Jesus' position is this: because people do not regard marriage with a high standard, divorce is easy to consider (see Matthew 19:3-6). The Pharisees pose their question not so much because they are really interested in the subject. Rather, they are simply looking for a contradiction in Jesus' teaching with that of Moses (see Deuteronomy 24:1-5). Most people divorce because of non-biblical reasons, such as poor communication, weight gain or financial problems.

Jesus understood marriage has a permanent relationship. It is important to note that God never demands divorce. However, God will permit or allow divorce. The divorce is permitted ultimately because of the hardened heart of a man or a woman (see Matthew 19:8). God allows divorce, the canceling of the covenant agreement. He does not demand divorce, nor did He create it.

God hates all things that threaten covenantal faithfulness. Marriage is the process by which two become one flesh. Divorce is the painful process of that flesh being torn apart.

That process might be managed well or poorly. If managed well, a person is able to continue with life's journey. If managed poorly, they become destructive and non-productive. Divorce in many ways is like a death. You must grieve the lost. "Divorced is not something you 'get;' divorcing is something you do."[21]

When a divorce occurs it is always helpful to consider why it took place and what role you may have played in the marriage dissolving. Most people who have gone through a divorce and are fearful of remarriage are those who have not truly analyzed what contribution they made to the failure of the first marriage. Divorce counseling is a great opportunity to begin the journey of analyzing why you married in the first place and what led to the divorce.

Divorce, like marriage, is a journey. It is not a one-day event. It is a long process toward healing and wholeness. I am proud to say that I have healed from that pain. I am on my second marriage. It will be my final marriage. Three years after going through the process of divorcing, I remarried. God has blessed me with a beautiful wife. I love Latron deeply, and we are happily making the journey into our marriage together. I love my wife and she loves me, and that is a great joy.

I learned a lot through the process of divorcing and remarriage. I learned that it does not matter if you have a thriving ministry if you do not have a thriving family. I learned that family life is the most important ministry. I learned that

---

[21] J. Randall Nichols, *Ending Marriage, Keeping Faith: A New Guide Through the Spiritual Journey of Divorce*, Wipf and Stock Publishers 2002, 7

you should not live a life that makes others happy but leaves you miserable. I learned that even pastors have pain, and that the pulpit has problems. Yet if God be for us, who can be against us?

REMARRIAGE

There is much debate concerning the issue of marriage, divorce and remarriage. Many look to remarry quickly after going through a divorce or the death of spouse. Others decide to remain single. The divorce rate among Christians is distressing. However, many Christians are trying marriage again, some for the second, third or fourth time. God realizes the fact that divorces will take place. Divorced or remarried believers should not feel that God does not love them or has eternally rejected them.

The modern-day church and specifically the Black Church must acknowledge the fact that divorce and remarriage is a reality and that ministries need to be instituted to help couples preserve their families. Many churches have programs such as marriage ministry. However, how many churches offer divorce recovery, singles ministry or a ministry that provides programming for women or men with unsaved spouses? The church should not be a place of judgment and execution. The church should be a place of grace and forgiveness. It is so hurtful to realize those moments when the church condemns where God forgives.

One of the most critical questions you must ask yourself concerning remarriage is, "Am I ready to be married again?" The reasoning behind why people choose to remarry is endless. Some choose to marry again because they are lonely. Some choose to remarry because they want to have children. Others choose to remarry because they think marriage will provide financial stability. Can I challenge you? If you want to marry because you are lonely, because you want to have children or because you think marriage will provide financial stability, those are the wrong reasons. Marriage may provide the opportunity for those things to take place. However, they should not be the reasons why you choose to remarry.

When counseling couples where one or both have been married before, I always ask them this question "Have you gained freedom from your previous marriage?" This is an important question, because whether we know it or not, our previous relationships have formed us. Previous relationships teach us to trust or not to trust, to share our thoughts or to keep them to ourselves. If you have not gained freedom from the previous marriage, it may cause difficulty in remarriage. What am I saying? Examine the baggage that you are carrying into your new marriage. Never lose sight of the fact that you are marrying a person with faults and failures, and so is your partner.

Life does not always provide us with the expected journey. With a new marriage comes new hope for the future. It is easy to imagine a new journey of home, peace, love and family togetherness. However, what I have discovered is that even with a new marriage, there are still unexpected turns that are made along the journey toward making a blended family work. For example: parenting styles, emotional baggage, relational expectations, communication barriers and conflict seem to keep you running around in circles as you seek to grow your family.

Remarriage is an opportunity to experience the grace of God. God loves blended families in the same way that He loves traditional families. Grace is God's way of reminding us that we are not alone. Grace is God's way of encouraging us to start again. It points us to the conclusion that God is still at work in our lives. God is in the business of redemption and transformation. Remarriage can be a beautiful thing if you allow it to grow in the grace of God. Relationships die when we fail to grow them in God's grace.

It is important that you understand remarriage does not heal you from the pain of divorce, emotional trauma from your past or any other negative experiences you have. "Just as the Israelites quickly found themselves caught between the Red Sea and Pharaoh's army, so stepfamilies shortly after remarriage find themselves caught between the future and the past."[22] Some people view remarriage as a second chance on life. Maybe their first spouse died or the relationship ended in divorce. Maybe they were never married at all, but have children from a previous relationship. Marriage, or in some cases remarriage, does not heal you from prior hurts. If you

---

[22] Ron L. Deal, *The Smart Step-Family: Seven Steps to a Healthy Family*, Bethany House Publishers 2002, p.18

are not healed prior to entering into a new relationship you bring those hurts with you. However, blended families are blessings from God. They take extra work. Nevertheless, there is a promised land to which wilderness wandering must eventually yield. There is grace to start over.

~CHAPTER FIVE~

BLENDING THE BLACK FAMILY

The focus on families, and particularly blended families, is important to me. I was born to an unwed teenage mother. The first ten years of my life, I lived with my mother and grandparents. I have never met my biological father. As a matter of fact, it wasn't until the age of about seven or eight years old that I even thought about his absence. I remember riding the elementary school bus one day. A conversation took place amongst the students. One of the boys on the bus asked me about my family. I told him that I had a mother and a grandmother. He asked about my father and I told him that I did not have a father. He responded by saying, "Yes you do. Everybody has a father."

It was at that moment that I began to realize I was missing something. Prior to this moment I did not sense any lack within my family. I had a great mother, a wonderful grandmother, a tremendous grandfather, who had passed. I had uncles and aunts and cousins. I never realized that I was lacking a father.

For me, it was normal not to have one. When I got home that afternoon, I asked my mother, "Where is my father?" I told her that one of the boys on the school bus told me that everybody had a father. She sat me down and explained that my biological father wanted nothing to do with us. Nevertheless, God would provide everything we needed.

A few years later my mother would meet a man by the name of Silas Hart. He had a son named Timothy Hart from a previous marriage. They would soon marry in the summer of 1985. I was ten years old. My new brother was six years old. My mother had a husband. I had a new brother. We had a blended family. This new family came with new lessons to learn. I had to learn how to share. I had to share toys. I had to share a room. I had to share my mother. It was an adjustment to say the least. We had a time adjusting to each other. We argued. We fought. We laughed. We cried. We wanted out. We wanted it to work. We had a time blending this new family structure. Needless to say, we made it. It worked. My parents are still happily married and in love. My brother and I are married with families of our own.

What is a blended family? A blended family, or a step family, is a family in which one or both partners have been married before, who have now remarried, in turn forming a new blended family that includes children. A blended family is also a family unit that has married with children from previous non-marital relationships. A relationship that begins in marriage without children is not a blended family. If there are no children involved the concept of blended families or step families is not needed. Blended families are those families where people are attempting to love children who are not biologically their own.

When my mother married my stepfather I understood the concept "stepfather." I understood the concept "stepbrother." However, I never really thought about the concept "step family" until I remarried after going through a divorce myself. Blending a family is a complex task, so much so that most professionals no longer use the term "blended" when describing the family agreement of our focus. They no longer prefer the term because they believe that blending is not the goal. Most professionals do not agree that one can truly blend a family. Blending, of course, refers to the process by which you combine ingredients into one fluid mixture, like a smoothie. The assumption is that each ingredient will relate to the others in the same uniform fashion. When it comes to family life, this is considered a rare occasion. "For example, biological parents and children will always have a stronger bond than stepparents and stepchildren, even if all goes well. And biologically related children will always have a tighter connection with blood relatives. This is not to say that different members of a stepfamily cannot be close. Many will develop deep emotional bonds, but there will always be a qualitative difference."[23]

I am not opposed to the term *blended family* because I believe blending is the goal. Even if the goal is never obtained, it is still the goal. "Not all stepfamilies have a difficult journey,

---

[23] Ibid p.64

but most will experience unexpected challenges. Some will face a great many barriers."[24] However, marriage is about commitment. When blending the family becomes difficult, we must remain dedicated to our vows and commit ourselves to them daily. Remember this: the problems that arise in blending the family are really distractions that keep us from focusing on what really matters.

A blended family is a family unit that has married with children from previous relationships. It is a family where people are attempting to love children who are not biologically their own. It is important to note that family ties existence beyond divorce. This is especially so when children are involved. Divorce simply rearranges family ties. It does not end them. For example an ex-wife is still a mother, and an ex-husband is still a father.

THE CHILDREN

Children often struggle with remarriage because it is a reminder to them that their biological parents are no longer in a loving relationship. They are often caught between the newly formed family structure and the family structure that previously existed. Counseling is always a good idea for children whose parents have divorced and are remarrying.

Children often find themselves wrestling with a conflict of loyalty. As a consequence, step parents work extra hard at

[24] Ibid p.21

becoming accepted in the life of the children. "Stepfamilies and loyalty conflicts go hand in hand."[25] The biological parent desires that the children and the new step parent get along. Therefore, there is an incredible stress and pulling on the part of the biological parent to make the new family structure work. For some families, this is easier said than done.

There are times when the children understand the desire of the biological parent. They understand that their biological mother or father wants the step parent to be accepted. However, they still seem to resist the step parent or even step siblings. When this happens, the biological parent often feels trapped between competing loyalties.

In order to sharpen your step parenting skills, it is necessary that you take the time to discern how the children might be impacted by the new family arrangement. Are they struggling with loyalty issues? Are they angry? Are they confused? Have they become distant? Talk to them and reassure them that you love them. Let them know that it is okay to still love the ex-wife or ex-husband, and that the new spouse is not a replacement for their biological family.

I strongly believe that in most cases, children want to love the new step parent, but they don't want to offend the biological parent who does not live with them. As a step parent, it is important that you never attempt to compare yourself to or intentionally try to outdo the absence parent. A word for the step parent, the relationship with the newly made step

<hr>

[25] Ibid p.110

children will develop at their pace and not at your pace. Don't take it personally; this is just the reality of the matter.

In my pastoral and even personal experience, the teenagers seem to have the most difficulty accepting the new family arrangements. This seems to be the case because teenagers are already exploring their own identity separate from the biological family. They are at the age where they are too old to do what they used to do, yet not old enough to do what they want to do. The pressure of accepting the new family while already desiring to be separate from the biological family is difficult for teens. If the relationship between the two biological parents is not one of co-parenting, it gives the teenager an opportunity to manipulate one over the other.

One of the hardest things to come to terms with is a teenager saying he or she no longer wants to live with you. It is heart wrenching when the child chooses to live with the other biological parent. In some weird way, it often is interpreted as another defeat in the divorcing process. As hard as it may be to hear those words, you must remember it is not about you. If you have experienced this, it is important to know that he or she still loves you. It is not necessarily a statement of rejection. You must remember that as a teenager, he or she is already detaching from the biological family and have very little interest in making a new family structure work. Give them over to God and continue to express your love for them. Be strong enough to hear what they have to say and pray about it.

So how should step parents interact with step children? Keep the lines of communication open. Communicating with children is not always easy, especially if they are teenagers. Become a better listener. Children are not capable of processing things at the level of an adult. When a child acts out or misbehaves, it is important that you interpret that behavior as a communication. The child may be having difficulty in expressing how he or she really feels about something. Therefore, because they do not know how to properly deal with what is bothering them, they act out their feelings, sometimes in destructive ways.

Do not play tug of war with your children. The Bible instructs us never to provoke our children toward anger (see Ephesians 6:4). Parents who continually go blow for blow with the children create more harm than good. Trust in the ability of God to do great things in your family. If you are thinking of remarriage or if you are currently remarried with children, consider the following as critical to your success in step parenting:

1. Make time for family prayer. Be intentional in including God into the process of blending the family.
2. Do the best you can not to show favorites. While you may have a closer relationship to your biological children, do your best not to favor one child over the other.
3. Do not require the step children to call you "mom or "dad." Doing so may cause unnecessary friction in the home.
4. Allow the biological parent to remain the primary disciplinarian in the child's life. This will aid in minimizing resentment or confusion toward the new step parent.

5. Never speak negatively of the absent parent.

6. Inform grandparents, aunt, uncles, godparents, etc., that gift giving should take into consideration the new family arrangement.

7. Never argue in front of the children. It is important the children view your marriage relationship as a healthy one. Do not give them reason to think this new family arrangement will lead to divorce as the previous one did.

8. Do not feel threatened by the relationship that biological parents have with their own children. Remember that relationship existed before your wedding.

9. Don't be ashamed if your family needs professional help in order to survive.

10. Have fun. Laughter has a way of healing hurts.

CONFLICT IS INEVITABLE

Conflict is inevitable. It is the natural consequence of living. As long as there is life, there will be some type of conflict and the need for conflict resolution. Sometimes conflict arises because people do not see eye to eye. Sometimes conflict arises because people have strong convictions about a thing. Sometimes conflict is rooted in arrogance or even ignorance.

Tolerance is an important word when it comes to family. Everyone has issues. Everyone has faults. Everyone has something that is less than desirable. The question is, do you have enough tolerance to maintain a healthy relationship? A successful family unit requires patience and a respect of differences toward each other.

Healthy conflict in families is a sign that loving adults and children feel anchored enough by their commitment to each other to air their differences. Jesus has given us the capacity to forgive ourselves and others. Where there is healthy conflict, there exist no spirit of revenge, the withholding of information or outrageous demands rooted in anger and frustration.

Successful families find a way to deal with a variety of issues. They have learned the art of fighting fair. What? That's right. Conflict is inevitable. Therefore, find a way to fight fair. When you find yourself in the midst of family conflict consider the following:

1. DIFFERENT DOES NOT MEAN DUMB

Do not be so arrogant to believe that if someone does not think like you, that they are dumb. Different does not mean dumb. No two people have the same fingerprint. No two people have the same DNA. People are different and have different backgrounds and different experiences. Just because someone may see things different does not mean they are dumb. Try taking the time to see the situation from the other person's point of view. You may realize that you are wrong and the other person is right.

2. DISAGREEMENTS DON'T HAVE TO LEAD TO DESTRUCTIVE BEHAVIOR

Too many times when people have a disagreement, what often follows the disagreement is unnecessary destructive behavior. There is no need to attack a person's character or seek revenge. Do not allow the disagreement to take you down a path of name calling and blaming. If you believe you have been wronged, let God handle it.

3. DO NOT BECOME PARALYZED STAY PRODUCTIVE

Never allow negativity to survive longer than it needs to. Make the best of a bad situation. The worst thing you can do in the midst of conflict is to become paralyzed by the pain and become unproductive in your living. Do something positive, productive and rewarding. You cannot always control what happens to you. However, you can always control how you respond.

~CHAPTER SIX~

I NEED GOD TO BLESS MY HOME

"The Lord's curse is on the house of the wicked, but he blesses the abode of the righteous." ~ **Proverbs 3:33**

There is dysfunction in every family. There is dysfunction in every biological family. There is dysfunction in every church family. As my pastor Dr. Sir Walter Mack said, "Every family has a Cain somewhere, a family member who will kill another family member. Every family has a Jacob somewhere who loves to take birthrights and other things that don't belong to that person. Every family has a Jezebel somewhere who exudes a spirit of witchcraft, control, and manipulation."[26]

I don't know the dysfunction of every family. I don't know the dysfunction of every church family. However, this is what I do know: every family has dysfunction. Maybe it is the dysfunction of addiction, abandonment or abuse. Maybe it is

---

[26] Dr. Sir Walter L. Mack Jr., Destined for Promotion Recognizing God's Plan to Move You Higher, Harrison House 2008, 104

the dysfunction of brawling, bankruptcy or betrayal. Maybe it is the dysfunction of being cowardly, confused or corrupt. Dysfunction is the human reality. If you are focused only on the dysfunction of the family you will miss the destiny of the family.

Here is something else I have discovered. While there is dysfunction in every family, every family member is not dysfunctional. There are productive family members who are a part of a family with dysfunction. Somebody in your family is doing better this year than he or she was doing last year. Somebody in your family is going to college. Somebody in your family is getting married. Somebody in your family is doing the best he or she can to make a name for himself or herself. This is the point that I'm making: don't be so focused on the dysfunction that you miss your destiny. Don't be so focused on your problems that you miss your purpose. Don't be so focused on your trial that you lose sight of your testimony.

It is without a doubt that many of our families are in trouble. Biological families are in trouble; and church families are struggling, as well. It should come as no surprise that the spirit of the enemy seeks to attack and attach itself to the institution of family. It was the institution of family that God created in the Garden of Eden when He called Adam into a deep sleep and took from his rib a bone and thereby made Eve, a wife and a help meet. Almost instantly, as soon as God created the institution of family, the spirit of the enemy began its attack. God established the family in Genesis chapter 2, and the attack on the family begins in Genesis chapter 3. It is clear to me that the enemy does not want to see families thrive in the glory of God, but would rather see families broken, wounded and damaged.

If we are honest, all of us would have to admit that none of our families are perfect. There is dysfunction in all families. There are arguments and disagreements that leave feelings hurt and bruised. There are family secrets that everybody knows but no one wants to talk about. Family life at times can be a mess. This is so because families are not perfect. Families are not perfect, because families are made of sinners and some are sinners saved by grace.

Many families are struggling with hostility, frustrations and stress that have their genesis in a number of traumatic circumstances. Yet God can and wants to make a big difference in the life your family. Psalm 127:1 says, "Unless the Lord builds the house, its builder labors in vain." A home must be built, and in some cases it must be torn down and rebuilt. The text before us says, "The Lord's curse is on the house of the wicked, but He blesses the abode of the righteous." Without God, we are nothing. Without Him, building the home or the church is a great mistake.

It has been said that one rotten apple can in fact spoil the bunch. The saying suggest literally that if you put a rotten apple in a box with other apples that the rotten apple will multiple itself and spreads quickly to all of them. There is an underlying threat to all families and that is the threat of rotten influences. Did you know that some people have an attraction to unhealthy situations and unhealthy people? We must always be cautious of who and what influences our thinking, our emotions, our relationships and the principles that govern our lives.

If we are not cautious of who and what influences us, it is possible to let other people ruin us. Association equals assimilation. Iron sharpens iron. Did you know that whomever you spend the most time with, you are most likely to become? Examine the company you keep. Examine the marriages that surround your marriage. Examine the friends that your sons and your daughters spend time with and remember association equals assimilation. If you surround your marriage with marriages that are not healthy, it is possible that their dysfunction may become your dysfunction. If you surround yourself with people who have bad habits, it is possible that their habits may become your habits.

One of the sad but true realities of life is that people who don't have a life, will often do their best to ruin yours. They are miserable, so they want you miserable. Their life isn't going anywhere, so they don't want yours to progress. They are hurting, so they want you to hurt. They are dysfunctional and they want to bring the dysfunction to your life. In the course of all of our lives, we are sometimes unaware and underestimate the damaging power of toxic people. We do not always realize that dealing with or associating with such people can turn out to be destructive. Yet some can testify that we have been exposed to some rotten influences and it was only by the grace of God that the rot did not spread to our hearts.

In my years of service in the pastoral office, what I have discovered is this, some relationship are ruined by outside influences. Can I encourage you? You are too gifted to let other people bring you down. God has provided and supplied your life with too much purpose to leave you without the opportunity to escape a rotten environment. You are too talented! You are too anointed! You have too much invested in you to let somebody who doesn't have a life ruin yours. Make the decision not to allow demons, devils or deviants to write your destiny.

If God be for you, who can stand against you? Too much has been given to you and your family. You must succeed. You must protect the investment God has made in you and in the lives of those you love. Your family is God's property.

As you grow in your gift, you will reach a point of utter frustration in sorting through the trash that other people bring to your door. Your gift refuses you to allow misery to be your medication, for negativity to be your need, for oppression to be your oasis and for problems to be the point that you pursue. You were uniquely created by God to fulfill a divine purpose. God provided your family an opportunity to fulfill a divine purpose. Do not let other people ruin your home. Don't let negative energy destroy what God gave you. Identify the toxic.

It is of the upmost importance to identify the toxic areas of your life. They must be identified so that you can create and maintain healthy situations, as opposed to settling in the toxic. In order to have a healthy and happy life, you must live in healthy and happy environments. In order to create the desired environment, it may require that you get rid of unhealthy friendships, unhealthy habits and even unhealthy thinking.

One of the greatest toxins the enemy uses to destroy families is unforgiveness. It is never too late to forgive. Forgiveness is a choice you can make at any time. You can forgive family members who have hurt you. Do not allow the enemy to destroy your family by allowing unforgiveness to live in your home and in your heart. It is toxic and cannot remain. Forgive so that you move forward.

The presence of God is the difference between having a blessed home and having a cursed one. It is also the difference in having a blessed church and in having a cursed church. The text also allows us to see that the wicked, He curses, and the righteous, He blesses! This means that God is active in all families. He is active in all churches, either blessing them or cursing them. And I don't know how you feel about it, but I don't want to live in a cursed home. I don't want to pastor a cursed church, but as for me and my house will we serve the Lord.

This text is critical because it allows us to see the reason why many of our families are in trouble. Many of our families are troubled because the favorable presence of God is not in our homes. In order for us to have the blessings of God in our homes and in our families, we must be willing to make a faith investment. Family living is a faith investment. We must invest in the long-term process of what it means to be a family. Look at the text; it says the blessings of God are in the abode or the home of the righteous. The question now becomes, what does it mean to be righteous or justified?

Justification means that there is imputed righteousness. We are righteous and we are justified, ultimately, because God said so. It means that God declared me righteous and declared you righteous. The text says the blessings of God are in the abode of the righteous, or the justified, or those whom the Lord has declared righteous. Therefore, the blessings of God enter into our homes because God wants the home to be blessed.

One clear sign of God's favor in your life and in the life of your family is the presence of good people. All of us need a friend to accompany us on our journey through life. Friendship can be one of the most wonderful gifts in the world. It was Cicero who declared that friendship makes prosperity more shining and lessens adversity by dividing and sharing it.

Friends are people to whom you can share bitter and sweet moments. They are people who will stick with you when nobody else wants to. I want you to know that has you travel through this life every now and then you ought to pray that God send you a real friend. A real friend is someone who will be there when all the chips are down. A real friend is someone who knows, but loves anyway.

Have you ever stopped to think about how good people are blessings from God? Have you ever thought about the support systems you have in your life? A praying mother, a strong father, a wise pastor, and loving friends are safety nets. They encourage the presence of God to remain in your home. They resist and fight against the plans that the enemy has for you. Every now and then you should thank God for your safety nets. God wants to bless your home and often does through the presence of good people and good friends.

God desires that the home of justified people be a blessed home. They are justified by their faith in God and the declaration of God based upon their life. Righteousness begins with faith, and then added to faith is knowledge. We may never have a perfect family, but we can have a better family if the family seeks to be a righteous family. When the family seeks to be righteous, the heart of the family attracts the heart of God. The house is blessed because God wants the house to be blessed. The church is blessed because God wants the church to be blessed.

~CHAPTER SEVEN~

THE BLACK CHURCH WILL SURVIVE

Preston Robert Washington, toward the end of the twentieth century, said, "The most important question facing the pilgrim people called Afro-Americans is, Will the black church survive?"[27] For many, life in the twenty-first century consists of complete busyness. We live in a fast-food culture that many have described as a Godless culture. With all of the happenings of our lives, who has time for church? In this postmodern era, an era that began in the 1980s and continued into the twenty-first century, more and more people are coming to the church without any biblical frame of reference. They do not know the difference between the Old and New Testament. Many of the biblical stories that are so familiar to those who grew up in the church are brand new for new churchgoers of this century.

---

[27] Preston Robert Washington, *God's Transforming Spirit: Black Church Renewal*, Judson Press 1988, 19

In this digital age of advancing technology, the message of Christ must be preached. We are not called to change the message of Christ. We are called to make the message of Christ attractive to modern hearers of the word, that they might become doers of the word. We currently live in a country were 1 in every 5 people has no religious affiliation at all. Many atheists are voicing their criticism of religion on mainstream media, as well as social media. How attractive is God in the age of Google?

The survival of the Black Church, in my opinion, is a matter of a discipleship. Being a disciple of Christ is more than just asking Jesus to save your soul. It is beyond your conversion and acceptance of the gospel. Discipleship is the process whereby you grow into deeper relationship with the Lord. As the church, we are called to be and to make disciples. This calling was given to us by Jesus Christ. We cannot ignore this calling. We must fulfill it. The goal of evangelism is to make a disciple. The goal of attending Bible study, Sunday school and morning worship is to make a disciple. Too many churches seem to focus their attention on membership and not enough attention to discipleship.

Church membership does not change communities. Discipleship changes communities. Being a disciple requires a conscious faith encounter with the power of God. Disciples are persons who seek to live obediently to God's will and God's word. I believe the Black Church will not only survive but it will thrive in the twenty-first century. I believe that dependence upon the Spirit of God, rather than secular business strategies, and a focus on discipleship, above the focus on membership, is the key.

In an effort to make ministry more attractive to busy people, the Black Church seems to be torn between relevant ministry and reverence to God. So many of our churches, and even our pastors, are so interested in being relevant to the culture, they have lost sight of the need to reverence God's presence. In some churches, there is more time allotted to community initiatives and community announcements than the word of God. Yet at the opposite end of the spectrum, there are many churches where the focus is so much on reverence that they are no longer relevant.

The challenge of ministry in the post-modern culture is the challenge of staying relevant but reverent. The Kingdom of God is about action, power and relationship. It is about knowledge and authority. As a body of believers, we have authority and power and the expectation is that we use it for the glory of God even while serving Him in a postmodern age.

What are modern day churchgoers looking for? They are looking for a ministry that honors the presence of God. They are looking for a church that longs for God's presence more than anything. The presence of God must be honored and desired more than large attendance, spacious facilities and popularly. God promises us in His word that He will draw close to us if we draw close to Him (see James 4:8).

They are looking for a ministry where they can grow into Word people without being there all day. As we focus on the 21st Century, we must consider the nature of the people to whom we are called to minister unto. We are providing ministry for people who have been socialized to be impatient. They love the Lord, but they will not sit in church all day.

They are looking for a ministry that can stay healthy. Even though modern day churchgoers are immersed into computers, cell phones, iPads and other gadgets, they are still craving meaningful relationships. Modern technology cannot replace the personal touch of another human being. We must never forget that the church is to be the salt of the Earth. People still crave meaningful relationships. The church is not a corporate organization. It is a living organism. It is the body of Christ. Resolving conflict is of paramount importance in the church. It is seldom easy, but it can and must be done. People are looking for a ministry that is both meaningful and healthy.

They are looking for a ministry where they can serve. People join the church because they sense that the ministry will make them a better Christian. However, they are also looking to join a movement. What movement, what causes, characterize your church? How is God's presence with your congregation making a difference in your community?

They are looking for a ministry they can trust. *Trust* is a key-word for ministry in the twenty-first century. In a postmodern world, there is a suspicion as it relates to authority. In order to minister Christ effectively, the modern-day churchgoer must trust both the message and the one who is delivering the message. Despite the falling away from the church, people still search for a ministry they can trust.

The Black Church will survive because it is all about faith and family. The Black Church is not simply a crowd of people that gather in a centralized location on Sunday mornings. For many, the Black Church is viewed as an extension of one's immediate family. This extension of family is what gives the congregation a sense of community. I'm the grandson of a pastor. I grew up in the pews of the Baptist church. As a result, I have many mothers and aunts and uncles who are not blood relatives. But then again, they are blood relatives. They are my mother, father, sister, brother, cousin, uncle and aunt in the Lord. As our churches grow in number, we must also grow in ministry. The only way to do that is to grow in relationship one with the other.

The Black Church is a community within a community. It is something unique about the fellowship of members of the Black Church. For many, particularly in rural America, the church is the only form of social, spiritual and intellectual stimulation. The radical experience of being Black and American makes the fellowship of the Black Church a unique experience. It is completely impossible to separate the Black Church from the Black experience. I cannot imagine what America would look like if it were possible.

The Black Church is a village. In the most traditional use of the word, *villages* are small groups of families who are situated together for sociability and defense. In the village, people look out for one another. In the village, there are many mothers and fathers. The village concept is such that the success of the individual is directly connected to the success of the group. Many

Black Churches function as little villages. We help each other. We support each other. There is a sense of safety that the Black Church provides to Black communities. While all Black people do not attend Black Churches, the majority of Black families appreciate the proximity of this institution within its village. It is all about faith and family. The Black Church, the black family, will survive if God be for us.

SELECTED BIBLIOGRAPHY

West, Cornel. *Race Matters*, Beacon Press, 1993, 2001

Booth, Charles E. *Bridging The Breach: Evangelical Thought and Liberation in the African-American Preaching Tradition*, Urban Ministries, Inc. 2000

Costen, Melva Wilson. *African-American Christian Worship*, Abingdon Press, 1993

Franklin, Robert M. *Crisis In The Village: Restoring Hope in African-American Communities*, Fortress Press, 2007

Cone, James H. *God of the Oppressed*, Seabury Press, 1975

Proctor, Samuel D. and Gardner C. Taylor, *We Have This Ministry*, Judson Press 1996

Massey, Floyd Jr. and Samuel Berry McKinney, *Church Administration in the Black Perspective*, Judson Press, 2003

~ABOUT THE AUTHOR~

*D*ynamic, relevant, uplifting and innovative are some of the words often used to describe the ministry of Dr. M. Keith McDaniel. A passionate preacher and teacher of the gospel, he currently serves as pastor of the 1,300-member Macedonia Missionary Baptist Church in Spartanburg, South Carolina. A native of Winston-Salem, North Carolina, he is a man who loves God and his family. He is an honors graduate of Shaw University, where he majored in religion and philosophy. He also holds a Master of Divinity degree from Duke Divinity School and a Doctor of Ministry degree from United Theological Seminary. He is a proud husband to Latron McDaniel, and the proud father of four children: Marceo Keith Jr., Savion, Madison and Kensley.

Dr. M. Keith McDaniel is also the author of *Live Your Kingdom Life Now: Theological Guide To Living By Choice Not By Chance.*

CPSIA information can be obtained at www.ICGtesting.com
Printed in the USA
LVOW04s2113240215

428192LV00011B/150/P